COR

CW01514652

WITHDRAWN

SMITH, A.J.
Cornish kitchen ware

0952873001

CORNWALL COUNTY COUNCIL
LIBRARIES AND ARTS DEPARTMENT

CORNISH KITCHEN WARE

BY
ALISON J SMITH

KELAN

Published by Kelan
5 Lyttelton Street
Worcester WR1 3JN
(Tel/Fax: 01905 21133)

© Alison J Smith 1996

Cover design © Davies Graphic Arts
Photographs © Ron Winwood
Page make-up by Townsend Ltd, Worcester
Printed by Ebenezer Baylis & Son Ltd, Worcester

ISBN 0 9528730 0 1

British Library cataloguing-in-print data
has been applied for

Typeset in 11/13pt New Baskerville

All rights reserved. No part of this book may be reproduced or
transmitted in any form, electronic or manual, including photocopy
or any information storage or retrieval system, without permission in
writing from the publisher

ACKNOWLEDGEMENTS

My sincere thanks to:

My husband for all his support and for all the miles we have travelled to find Cornish Kitchen Ware. Also I would like to thank my family and the following people for the help and support they have given:

.John and Athley Cowling, my friends; Helen McCabe of Peacock Publishing Ltd for the editing and preparation of this book; Wendy Cook, Assistant Curator, the Museum of Worcester Porcelain; Venetia Davies, Cargo Carpenters; Cloverleaf; Derbyshire Evening Telegraph; Derbyshire Studies Libraries for kind permission to quote from sources; Silver Street Antiques and Things, Cirencester; Worcester Antiques Centre, Reindeer Court.

ALISON J SMITH

Alison J Smith was born and still lives
in Worcestershire. She has collected
antique pottery and china for many years.
She is married with one son.

CONTENTS

1

INTRODUCTION

*W*hat is Cornish Kitchen Ware and when was it made? Where can you find it? I hope that this book will answer a few of the questions I am often asked.

I started collecting some time ago only to find there was little written information on the subject of this pottery and certainly no book about it. Hopefully, this publication will fill a gap in the market and in doing so, will be as enjoyable to read as it is informative...

The blue and white stripes of this attractive ware still sparkle after forty, sixty, or even eighty years. However, finding much information about the early days, in particular, was quite difficult.

At the beginning of my collecting, I approached many antique and bric-a-brac dealers with the question, "Have you any Cornish Kitchen Ware?" Invariably, I was met with blank stares. Evidently, they thought I was talking along the lines of butter, cheese and ice cream!

Further questions I directed to myself like, "Why was this pottery called Cornish Kitchen Ware?" or "Was it really made in Cornwall?" The lack of answers convinced me to research this book and answer them for myself and the growing numbers of other interested collectors.

Just looking at my fast-growing collection of colourful and cheerful pieces, it is easy to picture the idyllic scenery of Cornwall; blue seas, white sands, clouds and waves. In fact, I was getting nearer the truth than I imagined, *(see page 6)*.

Like other antiques, furniture, china and glass, this pottery has its own wonderful story to tell, but a favourite imagining of mine still remains - sitting in an olde-worlde

Cornish tea shop enjoying my cream tea served from a variety of sparkling blue and white pieces of Cornish Kitchen Ware...

Fig 1 *arrangement of tea ware.*

2

HOW TO RECOGNISE
A PIECE OF
CORNISH KITCHEN WARE

Cornish Kitchen Ware is immediately recognisable with the broad blue stripe on the white background. There is also a lemon and mustard variety, which is much less common.

Turn up the piece and you will see either a church or a shield on the bottom accompanied by the name *GREEN & CO LTD* or *T.G. GREEN & CO LTD*.

Feel for the slight grooves that the coloured bands make on the earthenware.

3

HISTORICAL BACKGROUND

*B*efore talking about the origins of Cornish Kitchen Ware it is necessary to think about the pottery process.

There have been potters since ancient times and, although production processes have increasingly become more sophisticated, one must begin with the clay and its shaper...

The potter kneads the clay to make it malleable and uses a variety of methods to shape it; the most sophisticated being the potter's wheel, which was invented in the fourth century.

Then the pot is fired in a kiln. In the process of firing, its composition is chemically altered and hardened and the type of pottery produced is determined by the nature of the clay and the way it is prepared; the temperature in the kiln and the kind of glaze that is used.

Earthenware, which is porous, is fired at a low temperature and turns buff, red, brown or black in the firing process. To decorate the fired pot, there are a variety of techniques, e.g. the pot is dipped into a slip, which is liquefied clay, strained of any coarse particles. The decoration of a piece with coloured slip and lathe turning is done before the first (biscuit) firing, which fuses the body of the piece with the handle and the decoration. The pot is then dipped in a colourless glaze and is fired a second time at a lower temperature...

Handling the comfortable pieces of my kitchen ware collection, I cannot help thinking of those early attempts at making and shaping and all the processes that led to the production of this striking pottery from which I have derived so much pleasure.

Just looking and turning a piece of Cornish Kitchen

Ware in my hand makes me think of the miners who dug out the clay for its manufacture and the coal to run the kilns for its firing. For this pottery was made initially for the working man and his family.

In the nineteenth century, much pottery was made in a number of small back yards and, with it, a variety of crude and common household and kitchen utensils. From the throes of the Industrial Revolution and the growth in population, jobs and wages, came a great demand for all consumer goods and, especially pottery. Hence the growth of a mighty industry.

Most people equate Stoke-on-Trent and Staffordshire as the centre for pottery making and especially creamware, which had been produced since 1754 when Josiah Wedgwood had experimented with its production and that of other coloured ware like red, basaltes, jasperware and the fine pearlware, which was cream with a bluish tint.

However, pottery was being made in Derbyshire too and a Derbyshire potter called T.G. Green was making money in the mid-1800's in a pottery factory at Church Gresley, which was built in 1790 by Mr Leedham and sold to T.G. Green in 1864. At that time, there was a great demand for white earthenware...

So from the privations and harsh working conditions of the pottery industry arose a different beauty; not the brittle fineness of porcelain but a sturdy earthenware used initially by workers and their families which, in its production, reflected their labouring skills.

Along with most collectors of beautiful and rare objects from the past, I derive my pleasure and my enthusiasm from seeing such skill and craftsmanship as a legacy bequeathed from the shapers, dippers, firers and painters of the pottery trade, who took just pride in their hard work and made full use of the elemental "earth, fire and water".

Originally, in the middle of the nineteenth century, most of the clay used at Church Gresley had been producing red and yellow earthenware. Owing to the great demand for white kitchen ware by both working class and middle class families, a decision was made to update the design. However it was felt that a cost effective and simple design only was needed.

You can imagine that not all pieces were completely finished on the potter's wheel and indeed, many were given variations of decoration by turning them on a lathe. These lathe decorations could be lines or beaded runners. It is easy to imagine the product emerging from the white-coloured clay and the process of manufacture, as a plain white pot turned into blue by slipping and the lathe then produced the blue and white stripes, revealing the broad, bright bands of colour that we know today as Cornish Kitchen Ware.

It is pertinent at this point to hint at how the pottery was given its name. Although this may not be quite the real answer, it is said that John Fanshawe, who was T.G. Green's South of England sales representative remarked, "The blue of Cornish skies and the white crests of the waves - let's call it Cornish Kitchen Ware..." I think, like the rest of us, its blue and white colouring evokes such memories!

However, the process of turning the pottery twice on the lathe was not only a skilled job but an expensive one. It also required a high standard of finish which was insisted upon by the firm. From this insistence on quality, this line outsold many cheap imitations that followed

Indeed, Cornish Kitchen Ware became extremely popular and in the early 1920s, the demand for matching dinner and tea ware provoked expansion into a wide range of decorative pottery and kitchen utensils.

During the Twenties and Thirties, when economics had begun to dictate social reform, the old-fashioned paid cook was being replaced by the fully-trained housewife! The latter knew exactly what she wanted for her kitchen, and expected her kitchen ware to be serviceable enough for everyday use but also to be practical and beautiful as well.

Bright and sturdy Cornish Kitchen Ware was the ideal choice to fulfil all her expectations.

In fact, for its modern appearance and clean look, the ware was given the award of The Royal Institute of Health and Public Hygiene in 1934.

Cornish Kitchen Ware was now finding its way from the ordinary working class kitchen to upstairs in the large city mansion or country house where Nanny and the children might have taken nursery tea from it and loved its sparkling brightness, or downstairs for the personal everyday use of the servants of the grand household. Services were bought for wedding gifts and it is interesting to speculate if any young couples who received it back in the Twenties and Thirties still own it today! However, many of the utensils produced were impractical and proved unpopular in the early days. Many have been found still lingering on shelves in old ironmongers' shops; items like global tea cups, rolling pins and early sugar sifters. Unsurprisingly, these have become extremely collectable and details of these will be found later in the book.

4

THE T.G.GREEN FAMILY

*T*homas Godwin Green was born in 1826 and was the son of a corn merchant and wharf owner of Boston, Lincolnshire. Thomas's father also operated a small fleet of steam cargo vessels travelling between Boston, Hull and Northern Europe.

Thomas fell in love with a lady by the name of Mary Tenniel who was the sister of John Tenniel, the cartoonist for *Punch* from 1850 to 1900 and illustrator of *Alice in Wonderland.*

Mary refused to marry Thomas so he decided to go to Australia where he set up his very successful contractor's business in farm fencing.

Some time later, Mary changed her mind and decided to accept his proposal so Thomas returned home and they were married in 1862.

When they were on their honeymoon in Scarborough, they met up with a potter by the name of Henry Wileman from Church Gresley, Derbyshire. This pottery had been built originally by Leedham in 1790 but Henry Wileman wanted to retire so he sold the pottery to Thomas in 1864 although Henry died shortly after the sale.

The address of where the factory stood was Pool Street, Jack i' th' oles, and is still known as this today.

History again doesn't tell us who *Jack* was but Pool Street joins up with a street called John Street. Could Jack and John have been local miners? Or one and the same?

The Old Works did have a pool of water around it and Pool Street joins up with Jack Street too. So were these two well-known men in that area? It is interesting to speculate...

Thomas did not have a great deal of capital so he returned to the traditional methods which then brought him success with a steady growth. In 1871, when the demand for Yellow Ware was falling, he realised a new product was needed. Therefore, T.G. Green decided to produce a new line in white earthenware.

The decision proved to be good as the demand for white pottery increased daily. So the search was on for larger premises.

Thomas, a skilled and forward-looking businessman, sank a shaft to a coal seam, constructed a brick kiln and then, by using his own materials and labour, built another pottery, which was duly called, The New Works. The roof itself was an innovation. Thomas used very heavy, pitch pine beams which were made by the company's own carpenters and pre-stressed during assembly.

The pitch pine beams were too large to be brought from Scandinavia in a ship's hold and so they were towed all the way to England.

A later alteration enlarging the Making Shops was no less ingenious as they jacked up the roof and then laid two to three courses of brickwork per day until they reached the desired height.

To be sure of an even lift, Thomas sat astride the ridge of the roof and, as he blew his whistle, all the workmen screwed the jack at the same time.

To help out on the administration side, Thomas brought in Henry William King and the business remained in the hands of the Green and King families until 1964.

In 1902, Thomas died aged 76 years. It has been suggested that he, personally, was not the man behind the origin of Cornish Kitchen Ware. In fact, little is known of who the real designers were. We can only surmise if it was the owner or his workers? Here we are reminded of the story of sales representative, John Fanshawe on holiday in Cornwall...

Unfortunately, in 1904, Thomas' death was followed by a disastrous fire at The New Works. But, afterwards, business continued as usual and then, in 1911, The New Works was updated by having electricity installed.

This work was carried out by Bellis and Moreton. Triple expansion steam engines turning Crompton Parkinson Generators were under the direction of Mr T F Raven, who was assisted by Mr H W Trefusis, the son of the Bishop of Crediton. However, H W Trefusis and his brother were tragically killed shortly afterwards in the Great War.

After the death of Thomas, the company was then controlled by Roger Green and Percy King, who were subsequently succeeded by their sons, Kenneth Stanley Green and Henry William King the Second, in 1924 and 1930 respectively.

5

THE PRODUCTION LINE

Fig 2 *mustard ware.*

*Y*ellow Ware continued to be produced in The Old Works. In fact, the pottery was the lemon and mustard variety of Cornish Kitchen Ware but was only manufactured for a time. The lemon line was produced for about seven or eight years only, while the mustard was made sporadically between the years 1920-1950 and probably re-designed in the Sixties and Seventies.

The Yellow Ware was much less popular than the blue. Therefore, owing to its selective production, it is a now a rarer find and more expensive. Its designs are quite different from the blue, e.g. the storage canister lids can be quite different.

Fig 3 *lemonware.*

Another line produced in Cornish Kitchen Ware is the domino variety - a wonderful blue with white spots. Again, a rarer find. It is interesting to note that the stamp on these pieces *(see Fig 10 page 17)* bears a domino with 10 spots (2 x 5). This pattern is repeated on each individual piece.

T.G. Green's white ware was produced in The New Works but after the First World War came a decline in demand, especially for items of toilet ware like wash bowls and hot water jugs.

During the depression which followed, prices were forced down and an eighteen piece decorated tea set was selling for just two shillings. This fall in prices precipitated such cutbacks as the two day working week.

These were the major factors which made T.G. Green's rethink and concentrate on their newly developing line, blue and white Cornish Kitchen Ware, which subsequently became a major product of the company for many years.

Fig 4 *domino.*

But a lack of information about its production processes over the next three decades probably resulted from the intervention of the Second World War.

Then, in 1955, changes in mechanisation in pottery manufacture, coupled with a 30% purchase tax, caused the company to slide into bankruptcy.

A receiver was appointed in 1965 and T.G. Green & Co Ltd was sold to a London finance company who appointed Mr T H Freeman to run the business; the outcome of which was that Cornish Kitchen Ware became a household name once more.

Sadly, in the late 1970's, the kilns were demolished although they were listed as an historic building site. Yet the Secretary of State for the Environment gave permission for their demolition so the factory could expand.

With any industry it is often the workers who are forgotten and it is significant that at T.G. Green's, a certain

Miss Clara Davis, who had worked at the factory for 68 years and never had a day's absence, was awarded the MBE. Clara retired on the 23rd December 1964 but was tragically killed in a motor vehicle accident shortly after retirement.

The last twelve cups that she made were to commemorate her retirement at the age of eighty-one and the inscription reads, '*A record service of 68 years as a cup maker at T. G. Green and Company Ltd. Church Gresley Potteries, 9th November 1896 to 23rd December 1964.*'

Another tragic end to what must have been a happy and fulfilling job. I am sure Clara took great pride in her work.

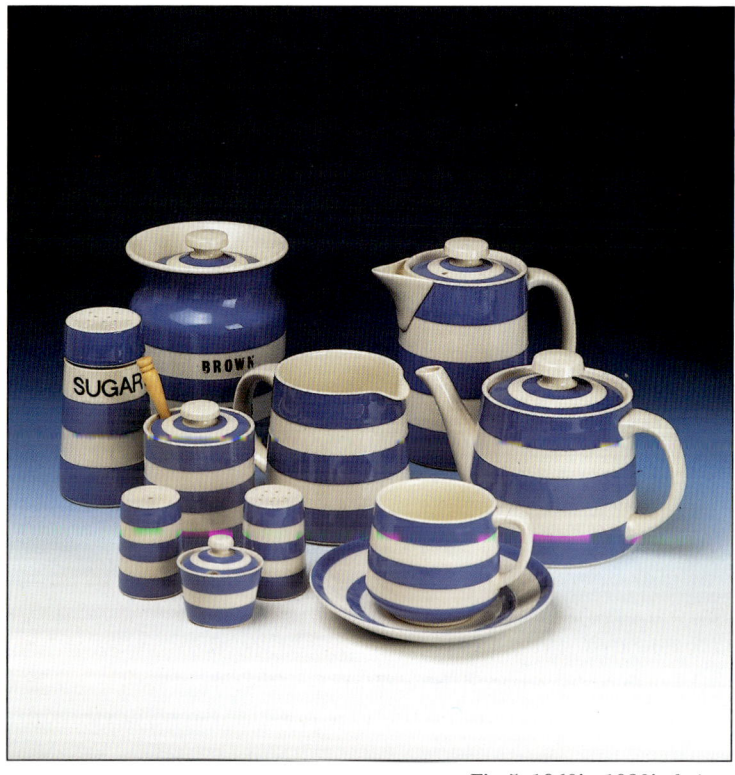

Fig 5 *1960's–1980's design.*

6

CHURCH GRESLEY AND T.G. GREEN

Why was the name *CHURCH GRESLEY* stamped on earlier pieces? It is a fact that Mr Leedham had built his factory in 1790 the same time as Sir Nigel Gresley was working a pottery at Church Gresley.

On the stamp, the *GREEN & COMPANY LTD* name over the church sometimes has the word *GRESLEY* below it. Although a professional partnership is not documented, it is likely some link existed.

We know that as far back as 1790, potteries were facing a variety of problems, not only having to survive economically but in the perfection of the production processes, e.g. trying to stop the glaze from cracking...

In 1794, the manufacturing of pottery was established in the neighbourhood of Burton-on-Trent, Derbyshire by Sir Nigel Gresley together with a modeller by the name of William Coffee of whom it was said, in June 1795, that he had given Sir Nigel, *'great satisfaction in his behaviour and business mind'.*

The factory was only fifty yards from Gresley Hall near the village and Castle of Gresley. Evidently, this project did not fulfil the expectations of Sir Nigel Gresley so, in 1800, the factory was passed on to Mr William Nadin but, indeed, soon proved to be another failure.

Nadin's own son recorded that his father had taken out a £700 fixed price for a dinner service for Queen Charlotte but this order was never completed.

It was evident too, that this particular pottery had to diversify; indeed, it produced not only porcelain, but china decorations for boots, shoes and slippers.

If Mr Nadin's son was correct, it seems unlikely that serviceable china was ever produced from the pottery.

After Nadin decided to discontinue the work, a Mr Burton of Linton continued for a few years until the pottery finally closed down.

Although a very ornate pattern is associated with the name *CHURCH GRESLEY*, there is no evidence to say that Cornish Kitchen Ware had anything to do with Sir Nigel Gresley or his pottery. An explanation could be that it was just to do with Church Gresley and not the Gresley family.

There is a standard decorative pattern (which is undocumented) dating from 1810-1820 but this had been used by several factories, therefore no one can be sure if Cornish Kitchen Ware was ever made here.

However, on the 7th May 1808, the notice of a partnership was published in the *London Gazette*. The partnership comprised James Rowley, William Burton and John Burton at Church Gresley. At that time, several potteries existed in the surrounding areas of Church Gresley.

7

STAMP MARKS

*O*ne important point to remember when purchasing any item of Cornish Kitchen Ware or any other pottery is the stamp. **ENGLAND** dates pottery around 1891 to 1899 and **MADE IN ENGLAND** from 1900 onwards.

(1) From two pieces in my collection, there appears here to be conflict in dating with regard to Cornish Kitchen Ware. It has been suggested that the ware dates from only 1918 but the spice jar pictured bears the mark *GREEN & CO LTD., GRESLEY, ENGLAND*. This suggests a date of c. 1891.

Fig 6 *spice jar* and Fig 7 *its mark.*

However, the cream jug bears the mark, *GREEN & CO LTD., GRESLEY, MADE IN ENGLAND*, thus dating it post 1900.

Therefore, we may assume Cornish Kitchen Ware was in existence pre 1900..

Fig 8 *cream jug* and Fig 9 *its mark.*

(2) There was also some good quality pottery which was made in blue domino, this mark having T.G. GREEN & CO LTD., BLUE DOMINO, ENGLAND.

Fig 10 *blue domino stamp.*

(3) This is a very unusual stamp. It has a church on it, with *T.G. GREEN & CO LTD.* surmounted and the word *CHURCH GRESLEY MADE IN ENGLAND* below. However, beside the church is a cloud or a tree.

Fig 11 *stamp.*

(4) If you are a collector you can usually tell if the pottery feels right just by touching it. Always remember that some early pieces were not marked or stamped.

A large quantity of Cornish Kitchen Ware was made in the 1930's onwards. One can tell this by the lettering on many

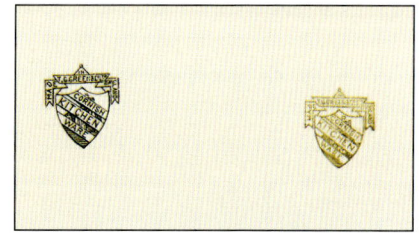

Fig 12 & 13 *shield marks.*

of the storage jars. The stamp on these is usually black, not green. As a rule, most pieces of kitchenware with black lettering has a black stamp. Many people know the shield mark which dates the pieces as 1920's to 1950's.

(5) The following stamp indicate pieces made in the 1960's, 1970's and 1980's. Again these dates are only approximate but at least you can recognise them.

(6) Modern pottery is slightly more creamy white than brilliant white and slightly heavier.

Fig 14 *stamp marks.*

Fig 15 *modern stamp.*

8

INDIVIDUAL PIECES

*T*he history behind many antique items is based on hearsay rather than concrete fact and, in the case of Cornish Kitchen Ware, where little is recorded, it is a surety that both the owners and their pottery workers have taken many secrets of its origin and manufacture to their graves.

It is a fact, too, that when workers at the T.G. Green factory went in to the factory every morning, it was decided what they would produce on a day-to-day basis, far removed from the computer-constructed and forward planning of today's manufacturing processes.

Rare Items

Fig 16 *rolling pin (and salt boxes).*

ROLLING PINS

Rolling pins are conventionally shaped but the difference is that when one used the rolling pin for pastry making, it left ridges in the pastry instead of leaving it smooth! The handles were painted blue, but some are plain. Consequently, these rolling pins became more of an ornament than functional.

SALT BOXES

Some of these are rare, the reason being that salt penetrated the glaze thus damaging it. It should also be noted that some were made with wooden lids and some with plastic lids. The wooden-lidded box is dated approximately c.1920, whereas the plastic-lidded piece, c.1950, although the stamp mark is identical.

Fig 17 *storage jars.*

LETTERED STORAGE JARS/STORAGE CADDIES

These come in all different sizes ranging from 20cm to 8.5cm in height. All have different lettering and varied lids – even a simple storage jar containing flour. An interesting point about the flour jars is that in the Twenties and Thirties, one added one's own raising agent to flour, whereas, in later years, the lettering on the jars designated 'self-raising' and 'plain' flour.

Fig 18 *pudding bowls.*

PUDDING BOWLS/LIPPED PUDDING BOWLS

Pudding bowls come in a variety of different sizes from one and a half pints to very small. The very nature of their use, which entailed standing them in boiling water for hours, makes them a rarer find.

Lipped pudding bowls, for pouring, of which there are many more around, have, nevertheless, sustained even more damage and perfect ones are rare.

Fig 19 *churn and milk jug.*

JUGS
Jugs come in a variety of sizes.

Fig 20.

DREADNOUGHT JUGS

Dreadnought jugs come in different sizes too. It is difficult to see how the housewife remembered each size, as only at a later date did the size appear on the bottom of the jug.

Fig 21.

DREADNOUGHT/PERCY JUG WITH COVERED LIDS

These do seem very rare. As you can see by the photograph there are two different shapes. What was it used for? I think the lid was made like a modern coaster. You covered the jug containing hot liquid and then when you put it on the table to serve, you took the lid off and placed it on the table thus using it as a coaster.

PERCY JUG

These again come in different sizes and a very slim style is pictured, c.1891.

Fig 22 *cream jug.*

CREAM JUG
This particular one my husband found and, to this day, I have never seen another one like it.

Fig 23.

MIXING BOWL/GLOBE BOWL/FLOUR/SALT SIFTERS
The globe shaped mixing bowl is very rare. These were well used for bread making and cake baking. c. 1891

FRUIT BOWLS
Large fruit bowl with rimmed edge dish and fruit saucer.

Fig 24.

TEAPOTS

I was not only lucky to find one round teapot (one and half pints) but then to find, as I call it, my 'baby' teapot (one pint), both shield-marked and in perfect condition. This was a best find for me. To find two has been remarkable.

Fig 25.

MUGS/CUPS AND SAUCERS/COFFEE POT/HOT WATER JUG

The global cups and saucers were modelled on a Royal Worcester design but were found to be most impractical as, when you poured hot tea into the cup, the cup wasn't deep enough and the tea shot back out. In fact, Worcester Porcelain abandoned this shallow wide topped shape in the 1920's as the tea went cold too quickly!

Fig 26.

CHEESE DISH/BISCUIT BARREL

The large cheese dish is an unusually shaped dish, which was often sold as a muffin dish. As for the biscuit barrel, it is doubtful as to whether the lid is correct, but the jar and handle is doubtless perfect.

Fig 27 *egg beater, egg separator, sugar sifters, pie/soup dish and vinegar bottle.*

EGG BEATER/EGG SEPARATOR ETC

The egg beater had been sold to me as a vase! I have only recently discovered this egg separator, c.1900-1930, which is all the more rare owing to its unusual stamp, that shows a cloud or tree, *(see fig 11)*. Once again, this item was impractical because it was not made deep enough as the white of the egg pours out of the slit.

Early sugar sifters have large holes in the top, c.1930. The smaller-holed, c.1950. Once again the large-holed is impractical because, as you shake the sugar, it pours out rather than sprinkles. The pie and the soup dish are both dated 1930-1950. The vinegar bottle is a rare find complete.

Fig 28 *yellow egg cup.*

YELLOW EGG CUP

Another item which I would like to add to my 'egg' collection, but which has eluded me, is the footed egg cup in blue. Although this isn't a small footed egg cup, it resembles rather a double egg cup but the larger side, if turned over, is too heavy. Perhaps an original use might have been as an egg cosy. However, the illustration above shows one in rare Yellow Ware.

Fig 29 *oval plate, cruet set, gravy boat and vegetable serving dish.*

OVAL PLATES ETC

The oval plate is an unusual piece as most plates are round.

The cruet set was a lucky find which comes in two different styles. The variation in shape denotes Dome, c.1920 (pictured).

This lipped gravy boat is an unusual shape as we usually think of a gravy boat being oval rather than round, c.1920.

This unusual vegetable serving dish appears to be based on a muffin dish design, c.1920.

As an avid collector, I have my favourite pieces of Cornish Kitchen Ware. These are three of the smaller items i.e. the cream jug, the egg separator and the one pint round teapot.

Although I have concentrated mainly on Cornish Kitchen Ware, I now cannot resist collecting any item with a *T.G. GREEN* stamp on the bottom. The company made a milk horn for the Great Western Railway; Coronation mugs and cups; chamber pots; jugs and basins; also other lines in kitchenware both in yellow and with a thin green border or line.

A couple of comments on the pieces I have designated as rare... There appear to be no oval pieces, which one might expect to be oval e.g. the gravy boat, (*see fig 29*) Most of them are round.

The most likely reason is that pieces which were oval-shaped were considerably more expensive to manufacture. Oval pieces cannot be turned easily on the lathe and, indeed, many oval-shaped pieces are lost due to warping in the kiln.

9

TIPS TO COLLECTORS

1 Check for damage. Although rare pieces may have some damage, you must use your own judgement when to buy, or not to buy.

2 Check for storage jars sealed with sellotape as this removes the glaze.

3 Look at stamps carefully as there is much variety.

4 Try to haggle a little on the price as every pound saved, goes towards your next piece.

5 Try to keep yourself to a limit on what price you are willing to pay. This I have found rather difficult!

6 You may pay a little more for one item and then find a bargain somewhere else so one counteracts the other. However, I have found if you hesitate there is always someone else who will buy.

7 If the glaze is badly marked, think about what price to pay and the rarity of the piece.

8 Some pieces have hairline cracks. Again think about price weighed against the fact of the manufacturing problems with most pottery in the early days.

9 Occasionally a few items are just very dirty, which is always risky. However, each piece cleans up immaculately with a little household detergent.

10 I would not advise washing any old pieces in a dishwasher.

I hope these are a few useful tips and that you continue to collect and enjoy every moment as I have. Always remember that rare item you are looking for is out there somewhere and will turn up when you least expect it to!

10

WHERE TO LOOK AND FIND

*T*he fun, as with any collectable item, is to go out hunting for it in antique and bric-a-brac shops, antique fairs and flea markets. Pieces of Cornish Kitchen Ware seem exceptionally difficult to find at car boot sales these days.

There is little to match the excitement of finding a piece of Cornish Kitchen Ware with no damage.

I have found pieces for which I have paid only five pence while the most I have paid to this day is £80 for a rare item.

As with any hobby you should try and keep yourself to a limit. And remember to keep secret what you have paid. It adds to the fun when other collectors are searching.

Always have a good look at all pieces when purchasing. Be extra careful with items that have lids on. The lids are often sellotaped to the top of storage jars thus taking off the glaze when the sellotape is removed. But you should always consider a slightly damaged (not badly damaged) item especially if it is rare. Pieces appear in all kinds of conditions. You may find one item with only a hairline crack, another very well used piece, then an item that looks as if it was made yesterday. I have been fortunate enough to find many of my pieces at:

**Silver Street Antiques
and Things**
9 Silver St
Cirencester
Gloucestershire
GL7 2BJ
Tel: (01285) 641600

Worcester Antiques Centre
Reindeer Court
Mealcheapen St
Worcester
WR1 4DF
Tel: (01905) 610680

11

POSTSCRIPT

*I*n the 1990's, potteries are still going into receivership. As I live in Worcester, I am also an avid collector of Worcester porcelain and, over the last fifteen years, have collected almost every item in the Evesham gold design. Recently, Worcester Porcelain has decided to change this design.

This compares with how Cornish Kitchen Ware continued to change to keep up with the customers' demands.

If you are a collector you very well know that collecting this pottery is becoming increasingly difficult and prices are at their highest. One speculates about buying trends. Is blue a fashionable colour at the moment? Is there a *Swinging Sixties* revival? Or has television prompted some of the interest? Could this simple and collectable pottery turn into another Clarice Cliff? Buying any antique item is always a good investment and through the recession of the Nineties, antiques have held their price.

The original purchasers and users of Cornish Kitchen Ware were working class people. Therefore, the rising demand for this simple pottery line, which was once commonplace and almost worthless, is most interesting.

The price of pieces has risen sharply and would have provoked open disbelief years ago.

We are now seeing the return of the pawn shop in many of our towns and cities. Doubtless, I shall be looking in soon and asking my favourite question, "Have you any Cornish Kitchen Ware?"

Where to find modern Cornish Kitchen Ware

*I*was so pleased to go into my local Cargo Carpenters to find a superb display of modern heat resistant and dishwasher proof Cornish Kitchen Ware. For your nearest branch contact:

Cargo Carpenters Homeshop
J W Carpenter Ltd
Thame Park Industrial Estate, Thame
Oxfordshire, OX9 3HD
Tel: (01844) 261800 (Head Office)
Tel: (01993) 778008 (Mail Order)

Sources:

Godden, Geoffrey A, FRSA. *Encyclopaedia of British Porcelain Manufacturing.* Barrie and Jenkins, 1988.

Derby Local Studies.

White, P M and Storer, J W, *Around the Wooden Box,* 29-31. J M Pearson & Son Ltd, 1984.

Cloverleaf, *The Story of Cornish Kitchen Ware.*

Collectors Notes